From Zero To Six Figure Sales With These Five Game Changing Strategies

Breakthrough Self Sabotage And Fear To Live The Life You Desire

Bill Feudale

Printed in the United States of America

© 2015 – Bill Feudale

Bill Feudale email – bill@beawinnerinlife.com

Website: www.beawinnerinlife.com

You Tube: www.youtube.com/channel/UCcBBgZ6y56gojlN1BkbXZ1w

LinkedIn.com: www.LinkedIn.com/billfeudale

Facebook: https://www.facebook.com/beawinnerinlife

Table of Contents

Acknowledgments

Among the many fine individuals who have helped make this book possible.

I would like to thank my wife Kelli,

To my friends Jackie and Jim Morey and the 90 Day Launchpad that they created to mentor authors. Jackie, you have been a blessing in my life and the life of others.

To Grant Cardone, although I have had many mentors in my life your material has changed my life and there is no way I could write this book without your influence on my material. Thank you Claudia Santiago for your support.

To my daughter Paige you are my biggest supporter.

To Hailey, you are the hardest worker and most dedicated person I have ever met.

To Mason you are what inspires me. To my Lord and savior, all the glory to you, for without you none of this is possible.

Dedication

This book is dedicated, with love, to my children,

Paige, Hailey and Mason Feudale.

Each one of you have taught me something about myself and inspired me to pursue my dreams and purpose in life.

Overview

Every day people are waking up and going to jobs that they don't like or want to go to, but they do. Why? They have a mortgage, a car loan, bills to pay. We are slaves to the middle class way of thinking. We were brought up to go to school, graduate, go to college and get a good job. Get married, buy a house in a suburban neighborhood and raise a family. Be happy with where we are, accept the fact that our childhood dreams aren't going to come to fruition. Be grateful we have a job. We work forty hours a week for forty years to live off of forty percent of our wages. We are trading time for money and money for time. I am always surprised when I greet people and I ask "how are you?" by the number of people who respond "living the dream!" Now listen, I am one of the most optimistic people you will ever meet, but that response is overused and a lie. Honestly if you are working forty hours a week in an 8X8 cubicle, living paycheck to paycheck making someone else's dream come true, would it not be fair to say you are not really "living the dream"?

The reason for me writing this book is I was actually living a life very similar to this and then I had a major health issue that really made me realize how short our time here is, and how I truly wasn't living my life, but just meandering through life so I could pay the bills. During this realization I came to the conclusion that I had taken for granted a lot of things that were very important to me and I also had many things I wanted to fulfill. I am a father and one thing that stands out to me is I really want to spend quality time with my kids before they are adults. I believe many parents today would say the same thing. That was a big one for me. Secondly, I have a passion for wanting to help others truly reach their purpose and potential in life without having to go through a major life crisis to get there. I believe that many of the readers of this book would have similar feelings about their lives. So if I can help you create freedom through reading this book, it is worth writing.

I have spent the last 13 years of my life in arguably the most brutal sales environment on the planet. Car sales! I am still in car sales even as I write this book. Although I do have a formal education, over the last 12 years I have learned more from the greatest mentors, cd's and books than I ever learned from a formal education. I have earned more money than most who have a master's degree and I actually could have done it with a high school diploma. I am not belittling a college degree but will say with the current cost of a college degree I could reasonably teach someone how to reach a six digit income and not pay six digits to get it. I am 100% confident that the content of this book will not only change your finances, but also your life.

I can't stop thinking of this interview I had with a young lady for a sales position and during the interview she said, "I am just not sure if I can do this." I said, "do what?" and she said, "Sales." My first thought was, young lady, you have been selling since the time you were four years old, you just don't realize it. You are constantly selling whether you know it or not. Whether it is a product or service, an idea, or just selling someone on liking you. Everyone needs to know how to sell or influence others to get what they want in life. Most people do not realize the importance of this skill in their lives and even fewer know the procedure in which to do it. One of the things you will learn is how critical selling is to your happiness and the five key strategies to get others to support and agree with you.

Look at any successful person and I can assure you that they successfully sold others to support them and their ideas to make it a reality. No success is achieved without getting others to support you.

Your ability to get others to believe in you will determine your happiness in life. Do you know how to persuade and influence others? Do you know the most important rules in selling? Do you know how to keep a good attitude even when things aren't going your way? Do you know the rule that if you help enough people, your dreams will become a reality?

You need to know these things in order for you to reach the goals in your life. The simple processes that I share with you I have learned over the past 20 years; this material I guarantee you will bring you freedom in your life. Be assured that every single day you are either selling or being sold. Your ability to sell others will ultimately determine how fulfilling your life will be.

If you learn how to sell you can go anywhere in the world and create income. You can have the freedom to do what you want, when you want. This book will help you live the life you have only dreamed of.

Bill Feudale

Chapter One

Poverty to Prosperity

"We live happily ever trapped if you just save my life/ Run and tell the angels that everything is alright.... "The Foo Fighters, "Learn To Fly"

I grew up in a small coal region in the foothills of the Appalachian Mountains. Shamokin, Pennsylvania was the name of city. My family life was in disarray from the start. My mother was 16 years old when she had me and my sister was born a year later. This was not good considering this was certainly not accepted in such a small Catholic based community where everyone knows everyone. My dad worked driving trucks for the coal mines and when he wasn't doing that he was also the local garbage man. I sometimes would go with him on Saturdays; I thought he was cool because he drove this big truck. My mom stayed at home caring for us kids. She didn't graduate from high school and had few work skills because by the time she would have been a junior she had two babies in diapers. Mom and dad separated when I was seven. My dad was so heartbroken over their break up that he drank every day. I remember waiting for him to pick us up on his days to have us and him not showing up. I would cry all night, I was so disappointed. I felt like he really didn't care about us.

About a year after they split up my grandmother found my dad in the bathroom throwing up blood. I guess he would drink close to a fifth of alcohol a night since they split. Unfortunately, it caught up to him. He was taken to the hospital and I never saw him again. I do remember mom getting a call from the hospital and she said the doctors said he was doing better and that we might be able to see him soon, and he passed away that night. I was eight years old and devastated by his passing.

Mom tried really hard to raise us properly but it was extremely hard as she was still a kid herself. My mother was very good looking, and I can remember people saying how much she looked like Loni Anderson; she was a very popular actress in the eighties who acted in a TV sitcom called WKRP in Cincinnati. It was a little awkward growing up in an environment where she still wanted to go out and party and all my friends' dads would hit on my mom.

She met a man who became her boyfriend and he was like a father figure for me for a time. He worked out of town and would stay gone during the week and come home on the weekends. Mom would go out during the week, sometimes leaving us to watch ourselves, while other times we had babysitters, some of which should not have been watching us. These were not good people and did bad things to us.

The sitters were better than a few of the adult neighbors who mom thought she could trust who ended up abusing us. I never really said anything as I felt guilty like I did something wrong, and these people told us if we ever said anything we would get into trouble. I suffered through many issues as a child because of all of these horrible things that had happened in my life.

Mom's relationship with her boyfriend was very rocky, to say the least. They would argue and fight, physical violence too; it was difficult. I remember he would sit and wait for her to come home from the bar, and most times I prayed that I would be asleep before she got there, but very seldom would I be able to do that. It was like our roles had switched and I was waiting for my child to come home. Then I was just relieved she was home, but then they would argue about her going out and partying till all hours of the night. Honestly, sometimes I felt sorry for him.

After many years of this it came to a head after a major argument; mom decided she was moving to Michigan to be close to her dad. She picked up and moved us. I recall I was in the eighth grade and playing football and she let me stay in Pennsylvania to finish up the season, and I stayed with my grandmother on my dad's side; it wasn't good, because she had no control over me. I got into all kind of stuff I shouldn't have.

I did move to Michigan after the football season. It was the worst experience of my life—Michigan in November when you know absolutely no one. I was so homesick I ended up going back to Pennsylvania to finish off that year. I came back that summer and never left. I played freshman football that year. I met a bunch of people and made a lot of friends.

We were poor; food stamps, government cheese. We used to put water in our milk to survive at the end of the month. The community we lived in was fairly affluent but we lived in a trailer park. I struggled with all of these different things but somehow I kept a good attitude. I had hope and confidence. Although my mom might not have been the best parent she did instill in me that I could be whatever I wanted, and she loved us and we loved her.

The next year I got a job. I wanted to have what the other kids had; nice clothes, a car, food. Looking back I wished I would have just worn old pants and went hungry, and rode a bike. However, I would not have become the person I am now without going through those things.

I worked the next couple of years while going to school. I was hanging out with the wrong crowd doing stupid stuff. I got behind in school and wasn't going to graduate with my class. I was a disaster; it was a disaster. I often refer to my life as the movie Eight Mile before Eight Mile. I didn't know how to sing, but I did know how to sell. I was sold on myself that I was going to be successful although at this point in my life I really didn't have a plan. I knew I had what it takes and I was going to prove everybody wrong. I was at one of the lowest points in my life and that is when it all changed.

Look at your life and all the things you have had to go through to get to where you are today. Life is grand when things are going your way, but how do you react when things aren't going your way? I know for me going through these things in my life taught me a lot about myself. I was grateful for everything I had; I know I would never have become the person I am today without these tough life lessons that I learned as a child. I know there were times I felt I was a row boat in the ocean of life but I had faith, and I believed that I could become somebody and achieve things that no one else in my family had ever achieved.

I was going into my fifth year in high school. The one good thing that happened was because I started school when I was four I was eligible to play football that year, and that was very important to me. I was dating a girl whose father was a mentor to me. He used to ask me, "Son, what are you going to do when you grow up?" He asked me this every day. I told him I was going to play football, finish high school, go to college and start my own business. I told him that every day. This was an important life lesson and I wasn't even aware of it at the time. Your brain is the most amazing organ in the body. The cool thing is when you learn how it works you can actually program it to work for you. What I was doing daily by telling her father what I was going to do with my life is programming my mind to believe it. A thought remains a thought or an idea until you speak it or write it down; then it becomes a goal.

I played football that year and I was a beast. I had so much fun. I graduated from high school, and I ended up getting a partial scholarship through the adult education program as I was taking some college prep classes along with my high school classes. I went to college and graduated with an Associate's Degree in Business Management and Marketing.

I started an auto detailing business at the end of my college courses. It was a brick and mortar business that I owned for five years. I gave the business up because after five years my employees were making as much as I was. I would often say if I could get back into business without all the overhead of a brick and mortar business, I would do it. I believe all of this came to pass because my girlfriend's dad was mentoring me. By asking these questions every day I was training my mind to believe these things would happen. This was a monumental breakthrough in my life. I will touch more on this subject in a later chapter in this book.

I went to work at one of the dealerships I was doing work for. One of the things that made my detail business successful was I knew no one had a better process for cleaning cars than I did. I took that same process to the dealership and was very successful and profitable. I ended up making $40,000 in my last year as a detailer. I thought that was very good for a detailer at a car dealership. But my goals were much greater than that. I knew to reach my potential I would need to do something different than detailing cars.

While I was growing up my mom would always say you could sell an Eskimo ice! When I was detailing cars everyone would tell me you should be selling cars instead of detailing them. I was always nervous about going into sales. Car sales always had this negative connotation. If you grew up in the 70's and 80's like I did you might remember the sitcom Three's Company with Suzanne Sommers. Well their neighbor in the show, Larry, was a car salesman and he was portrayed as a fast talking, swindler type guy. That is the image that came to my mind. I believe that even today people think of car salesmen in this way.

I remember the day I decided I was going to take the leap into sales. I had actually tried sales once before but wasn't mentally committed to making it happen. I was on my way home from the hospital after my second child was born and I was overwhelmed with the thoughts of responsibility when I realized no matter how hard I worked or how many days of vacation I gave up, I could only clean so many cars. I realized I was pretty much capped out on the money I could earn detailing cars. I knew right then that I needed to move into sales and because I was in the car business, car sales it would be.

I was working at a dealer managing their detail department but I interviewed with several other dealers about sales. The irony to this story is one of the dealers I interviewed with that I really wanted to work for would not hire a Green Pea. Green Pea is a term used at dealers for someone without sales experience. So I worked into a sales position at the dealership I had been at and in my first year I became the number two salesman at that store. I remember I sold 100 cars and made $54,000. I was turning in my car at the dealer that I wanted the job at that wouldn't hire a Green Pea. They had heard I was now selling and had some success and they offered me a job. I took the job mainly because they sold General Motors products, which was very prevalent where I lived in Michigan. I remember working my first week at the new dealership and my old boss was calling me and I was really struggling with my decision. I had to learn an entirely different product line, and this dealership had many more consultants. I went from a big fish in a small pond to a small fish in a big pond. I was sitting in my car debating what to do, and I still had my box from the other dealership sitting on the seat; I hadn't even unloaded it yet. It dawned on me while contemplating what to do that it wouldn't be fair to me, the new dealer or my previous dealer if I didn't stick to my decision. I went in and sold my first car that night. Those people who bought that car are still clients of mine to this day.

My goals were to be the number one consultant at this store in less than 5 years. I felt like, "Just wait until I really know what I am doing." I say this because other than wanting to be a customer advocate, someone my customers could trust and believe in, I really had no actual sales training. I knew the products and I was friendly and worked hard. An Olympic gold medalist didn't win the gold without training and I felt like I was missing critical pieces to reach my potential.

I was averaging about 8 cars a month and was in the top half of the sales consultants at our store. I was in my second year at the store and had sold 154 units in my first year. I was doing okay but not really moving up any further. I met a promoter from Detroit; his name is Bob Mohr. He was promoting a sales seminar that was going to be held locally in a few weeks. I decided to take him up on his offer. I went to his seminar and met the second real mentor of my life; his name is Grant Cardone. I knew there were people selling like I was but he took it to a different level. It was a total 360 from what I had ever seen before. I really did not know there was a method to handling customers and their objections in a total soft sell approach to sales. I went from an 8 car a month guy to a 16 car a month guy in less than a year. I read every book on sales and listened to all of Grants cd's. I became obsessed with this material and quite frankly, it changed my life. I reached my goal of being the number one consultant at our dealership in my fourth year, one year ahead of my projection. I was the number one consultant for two years in a row. The dealer than asked me if I would be interested in management and I became a manager. I served in that role for several years. I then became a corporate trainer for the group. Ultimately I landed my dream job; I became a General Sales Manager at a store of my own.

I was a six digit earner and I had reached my dream job, but a funny thing happened. The dream job turned into a nightmare. I was working six days a week, a two hour drive daily and 10 hour days. I never saw my kids. I had never felt like this before but now I dreaded waking up in the morning. I was stressed out all the time and I was finding it hard to smile. I had worked so hard to get to this point in my life, and I finally get here and now it isn't what I had thought it was going to be. I decided to go back to sales and after one year at my own store I moved back to sales. When I moved back to sales I had a more flexible schedule, one that allowed me to become a football coach for my son. I will tell you it has been one of the most rewarding things I have ever done.

I was working in sales and about 9 months after being back I suffered a heart attack. Although I made it through this, it had a profound effect on my life. I realized how precious our time is here. Find what you are passionate about and it will never feel like work. Live everyday like it is your last.

Most importantly, I could sum up this chapter in a brief analogy that I heard from Joel Osteen. "The next chance you get when you sit in your car look at your windshield compared to your rearview mirror. The windshield is so much bigger than the rear view mirror because what is in front of you is far more important than what is behind you."

In the next 5 Chapters in this book I will share with you the Game Changing Strategies that took me from poverty to prosperity. I am so confident this material is so powerful that it will not only change your finances, it will change your life, that I will guarantee a 100% money back offer if you are not completely satisfied.

I can't share everything I have learned over the past 12 years of studying this information in this one book, but I plan on having a series of books to follow as well as an online course. I also plan on producing a series of videos for this book that coincide with each chapter.

"Like a small boat on the ocean/ Sending big waves into motion/ Like how a single word can make a heart open/ I might only have one match/ But I can make an explosion..." Rachel Platten, "Fight Song"

Chapter 2

The Selling Essentials

"A sale is made on every call you make. Either you sell the client some stock or he sells you a reason he can't. Either way a sale is made, the only question is who is going to close?" From the movie "The Boiler Room" (2000)

I n this chapter I will not only define what selling is, but why it is critical to your happiness. I will also break down our fear of sales and how to overcome it. I will deliver critical information on how to change your mindset so you can change your outcomes and achieve life's greatest rewards.

Selling as defined by the dictionary is, "To give up or surrender in exchange for a price or reward." I love this definition, and who does this apply to?

Selling affects every single person, every day. Your ability to influence, persuade and convince others of your thoughts and ideas and your position in life will ultimately determine how successful your life will be.

The more consistency you have in selling people to like you, to work with you and to want to please you, the happier and more rewarding your life will be. In every transaction of ideas with another person or group of people you are either selling or being sold. You have more experience selling than other assets. You have been selling since you were born. Even before you were able to speak you cried when you were hungry so someone would feed you. Kids are the greatest salespeople in the world! Picture the last time you were at the grocery store and you're in line and the kid in front of you is asking for candy in the aisle and the mothers says, "No Johnny, you can't have that." Johnny says, "Momma, please momma, momma please!" Johnny won't take no for an answer; he is relentless until mom finally gives in. How many times have you seen this happen or experienced it yourself?

I mentioned that I loved the definition given above for selling, to give up or surrender. Would you agree that the mother in the story above just gave up and the reward for Johnny was the candy? I believe some of life's greatest rewards have nothing to do with money. In order for you to get married you had to convince your wife you were the one. If you want to have children you have to convince your spouse that you would be a good father. If you want a promotion at work you must convince your boss you are worthy of that promotion. Every time you get your way, you have been paid commission.

Understand everyone in the world is involved with selling. You're selling virtually every minute of every day, in one way or another. If you have a negative connotation of selling, you think of some fast talking, high pressure sales guy. You have been programmed with these negative images but in no way do they represent a professional salesperson. A professional salesperson conducts himself with the highest integrity and persuasive skills so that he doesn't have to resort to pressure or confrontation to get his way.

I am constantly surprised at the number of people who can give a referral for a person or business and get paid absolutely nothing for the referral, but if they were being paid to refer a person or business they can't do it. I believe this is because we are programmed that sales is negative.

Regardless of your preconceived programming of what sales and a salesperson is, you must adhere to the fact that you will have to sell no matter what your situation is in life. There is no exclusions to this rule. I am a youth football coach and if I can't sell my team on my way of coaching and our play calling, I will not be successful. My success as a coach depends on my ability to sell the kids on me as their coach. This analogy works in any role you have in your life, whether it is a paid or volunteer position. Selling is vital to your success in life!

The things that I am teaching you are not taught in school. I have a formal education but I can honestly tell you that I have learned more from books and cd's than I ever did in my formal education.

From the cradle to the grave you have been selling your entire life; what are you so afraid of?

There is only one natural fear you are born with, and that is the fear of death or bodily harm. Every other fear you have created. Many fears are conceived from past experiences or fears from your childhood, some fears may have been produced in your subconscious even before birth. "Fear and self-doubt plague all of us. To the degree you can overcome your insecurities, you will experience freedom to be yourself and reach your full potential"... Grant Cardone, the author of The 10X Rule.

Why are so many people afraid of sales or selling? In my overview I mentioned the girl I was interviewing who said during the interview, "I'm not sure I can do this." And I said, "Do What?" and she said, "Sales!" I wanted to tell her you have been selling since you have been 4 years old and just didn't realize it. Selling people on your thoughts, ideas, and wanting them to like you. So why this fear of selling? I believe it is a lack of knowledge and fear of rejection and failure.

I gave the analogy of me being a youth football coach. If I was not knowledgeable about football, would I be a successful coach? If I wasn't having success coaching, would I be inspired to continue coaching? Probably not. Generally if you are unsuccessful at something you lose the desire to continue whatever it is you are doing. A sales consultant who can't sell won't like selling. Knowledge is the greatest commodity you can own. Knowledge is power. How do you gain knowledge? You train! I have been training in the art of selling for over 12 years of my life. The Olympic Gold Medalist did not just show up at the Games and win the Gold; that achievement was created in the countless hours of training when no one was watching! If you gain the knowledge through training you will be able to predict your income, your outcome and your life.

I need to define knowledge; in the sense of being a football coach if I just coached the basics of football to my team and even if I was the very best, I can assure you I would not be nearly as successful as I would be if I taught the basics of football and found out what motivated my players. In sales, no matter what the product or service being sold, your knowledge of the product or service would only make up 15% of the sale. Your attitude, enthusiasm, smile, body language, and knowledge of what INSPIRES your customer to buy will affect 85% of every sale. I am not saying that product knowledge isn't important, however to be a professional in sales you must master all of these aspects.

A great example of this is anyone in sales currently probably has heard of the 90 day phenomenon. This is where a new hire with very little experience in sales is one of the leaders in his or her first 90 days. Why is this? The new hire doesn't know any better, so their attitude and enthusiasm is unaffected by the outcome! After 90 days they start forming opinions and pre-judging their clients; they're programming changes.

Change Your Programming, Change Your Life

No book, coaching program, or motivational seminar will ever have a long-lasting impact on your life until you understand the concepts I am about to reveal. I used to wonder why, after a great sales seminar, that after a few hours, a few days or a few weeks I would lose that motivation that had been created at the seminar.

I figured it out after reading a book titled, "What To Say When You Talk To Your Self" by Shad Helmstetter. What I learned is your programming creates beliefs. Your beliefs create attitudes. Your attitudes create feelings. Feelings determine actions. Actions create results. If you want to change your results, you must change your programming.

We believe what we are programmed to believe. Our conditioning from birth has created, reinforced, and cemented most of what we believe about ourselves. Whether it is right or wrong, the result of it is what we believe. God did not create you to fail, so why then are some people more successful than others? I believe it is based on the programming that has occurred in a person's life, much of which, by the way, is incorrect. If from birth until you are 6 years old you have been told no not to do something over 150,000 times, do you think your mind is wired not to do this particular thing? Would it limit you? If your parents told you while you were growing up that you would never amount to anything, and you heard this hundreds of times, what impact would this have on your self-esteem? You would believe that you will never amount to anything.

If you logged all of your self-talk for the next week, what would it look like? What if you took the most successful person you know and were able to log his or her self-talk? Then take the biggest failure you know and were able to log their self-talk? If you were able to compare their self-talk I can assure you that would be the difference in success and failure.

The good thing is you can change this by implementing new programming. Neuroplasticity refers to the brain's ability to reorganize and change new neural pathways to adapt to meet our needs. Whatever we do or think repetitively creates a neural pathway in the brain, much like a groove in the road. It is the same way your negative programming was created.

It all starts with programming. What we have accepted from the outside world, fed ourselves, been taught by our parents, has initiated a cause and effect chain reaction which will lead us to successful self-management, or unsuccessful mismanagement of ourselves. The antidote for your programming is positive self-talk, visualization, and positive information repeated for a duration of time.

Picture your mind as a home and all the negative thoughts in your mind are broken down pieces of furniture in your home. One day you decide to get rid of all the broken down pieces of furniture (negative thoughts) and you spend all day taking the broken down furniture to the garage. Now you're hungry and decide to eat but there is nowhere to sit; what do you do? You start grabbing the broken down furniture from the garage. Before you know it all the broken down furniture is back in your house. That is why I couldn't stay motivated after that sales seminar; after a short period of time I went back to my old programming. What you need to do is replace the old furniture with new furniture, and that would be positive thoughts.

I want to take this even further. So let's say you wanted to lose weight. I would recommend you wake up every morning and start telling yourself you enjoy eating healthy food, start telling yourself how great you feel after working out. I would take 10 minutes in a quiet spot daily and visualize yourself being thinner; I would put a picture of yourself from when you were thin on your bathroom mirror where you get ready in the morning. I would also put that same picture in your car, your wallet, your purse. In the car, on your drive, talk positively to yourself about your weight loss. Listen to something positive in your car. I will guarantee in 30 days you will see results. You could do that with smoking. If you wanted to improve your sales, listen to a sales training cd and do it every day and you will become an expert on that information on the cd. Repetition is the key, repetition, repetition, repetition.

The ripple effect of this is if you change your programming you will change your beliefs, your attitude and your feelings. Your feelings will determine your actions and your actions will create results! Think back to Chapter One when I spoke of my first mentor; my programming changed because my thoughts changed on my future. SPEAKING it brought my thoughts to life. This changed my attitude towards what was upcoming in my life. This forced me to take action, which led to my results.

Two things changed the first time I hit my goal of being the number one sales consultant at the dealership I worked for.

First, I had been listening to a cd by my mentor Grant Cardone. I had listened to this cd every day for almost a year and it was about attitude. Repetition is key. I remember distinctly I used to sit at my desk in a high traffic area and would just smile and shake my head yes all day long. I looked like a freaking bobble head on steroids. When I got a customer I said yes to everything; my attitude was no matter what the customer said, I was just going to say yes and smile. It was amazing the results I got by simply practicing smiling and shaking my head yes. The repetition of listening to the cd and practicing changed my programming, beliefs, attitude and feelings, which led to me leading the dealership in sales.

Secondly, I accepted rejection and failure. I realized these feelings were normal. I knew if I was to reach my full potential I had to step out of my comfort zone to do it; I had to stretch myself or else I would be stuck in mediocrity. Every month that I led the store in sales, I also led the store in the number of people who said no.

I embraced failure! I believe failure breeds success. Every great thing that I have achieved in my life came after I had failed. Failing or losing at something makes you hungry and it causes you to work harder. I remember as a manager at the dealership giving a speech to the staff where I challenged them to go fail! The more you fail the more you will succeed if you use it to learn and motivate. You will either quit from your lack of success or you will figure out what it takes to be great.

"The most important persuasion tool you have in your entire arsenal is integrity." Zig Ziglar

Chapter 3

Be Prepared

"Before anything else preparation is the key to success."
Alexander Graham Bell

I n this chapter I will walk you through the steps to success in sales. Most salespeople fail in sales because they are unprepared. I will give you all the necessary information for you to be educated on what it takes to be great in sales. No matter what you are selling, from retail sales to multi-level marketing or just getting your own way, this knowledge is crucial to your progress.

Your Greatest Sale

You will never have success at selling if you are not 100% sold on the product or service yourself. This rule is non-negotiable and is essential to anything you will ever sell. Your success in sales is determined by the degree at which you are sold. If you're not selling, you are not sold. Your sales are lagging, you're not sold. You are not getting what you want, you are not sold.

You must sell yourself completely that your product, service, or ideas are superior to all others in the market. If you want to be great as a salesperson, this is the most important sale of your entire life!

I believe you must be obsessed with the fact that your product or service is so exceptional that any other option would be ludicrous. That others may have similar benefits to yours; you must be convinced that what you're selling is greater than all options.

I recall early in my sales career I was working with a customer on a vehicle that I felt was overpriced. When we got to negotiating, the customer's objection was price. I could not overcome the customer's price objection because I believed the car was too expensive. How could I ever convince him that it wasn't? What I later realized was I believed it was too much money because I was not aware of all of that car's features and benefits. When I was fully trained on the features and benefits of that car, I was easily able to overcome the price objection.

Your perception is your reality. What you believe, you will make come to fruition. When I first got started in the car business there was a saying that "buyers are liars"! I never believed this to be true however I did find out what they meant by this saying. Buyers are not liars. If I see a customer walk in the dealership and I prejudge him or her, I will make that come true because my need to be right is more important than anything else. I developed a total soft sell approach to selling in which when I greet a customer, I have no prejudice. If I would have bought into that saying and greeted a customer that I felt was a liar, I would have asked him questions that would have forced him to lie to me. Here is an example in greeting a customer. If I asked the question, "do you have a budget in mind for your car purchase?' The answer to this question has been the same for the last 12 years: "$250 with no money down!" Realize the customer is looking at a $50,000 dollar car that they have been pricing online for the last two weeks. They know that is not possible but if you ask a stupid question, expect a stupid answer. Buyers are not liars, stop asking stupid questions!

You must be relentless in your belief in your product or service and be able to demonstrate this to your customer with complete confidence so that they feel like there are no other options. The degree in which you demonstrate this will determine your ability to sell.

Attitude

Attitude is the single most important thing you can control. When I was younger I did not realize that my attitude was up to me. Attitude trumps all other things including failure or success, education, money and what people say or do. It is more important than talent or skill. Every day we determine our attitude for the day. We can't change the past or things that are out of our control. However we can control the way we react to the things that happen in that day. Listen, if you wake up and tell yourself that it's not going to be a good day. I can assure you it won't be a good day. If you wake up and tell yourself it's going to be a good day you will make it a good day. This doesn't mean things won't happen in that day that are not good but it is how you react to those things that will determine the outcome of the day. You are the only one that controls your attitude.

I have studied successful salespeople for the last 12 years and every successful person I have met or came in contact with has a great attitude. I have made over $100,000 dollars on attitude. I have sold cars on my attitude alone. It is contagious. Remember you can control your attitude 100%. I didn't realize this until I was in my mid-twenties. I thought attitude was a feeling. Attitude is a choice! Programming creates attitude; change your programming by positive thoughts, self-talk and visualization.

Attitude can be taught because it is a choice you make daily. Start by smiling. Do you know what happens when you smile at someone? Most times, they smile back. Even if you are not someone who smiles, start smiling. Smile every day at as many people as you can. Look them in the eyes, be genuine. Shake your head yes and smile and watch the reaction from the people you are greeting. Don't read the newspaper, stop watching the news, and find something positive to listen to when you are driving, read positive books, and start talking to yourself positively daily. I challenge you to do this for 30 days and watch the difference you make in other people's lives. Repetition is the key to changing; do these things daily for 30 days. Think of it like taking vitamins; you can't take one vitamin and expect results, you must take the vitamin daily. You must break down your old programming daily and create new programming, and this will take about a month. You will literally have friends and co-workers asking "What happened?" You will attract people to you, and you will reap what you sow!

"We all need a daily checkup from the neck up to avoid stinking' thinking'," said Zig Ziglar. Before every customer I would do a checkup from my neck up, to make sure my attitude was solid. If my attitude was not good I would give the customer to someone else because if I have a bad attitude it will definitely rub off on my customer. If I was feeling down, or depressed over a deal I just lost, probably not the best time to take your next customer. I learned to get over those deals so they did not affect my attitude with my next customer.

Every great salesperson I ever met also had an attitude of gratitude! Be grateful, stop worrying about what you don't have but be grateful every day for what you do have. I used to be thankful that the dealership had millions of dollars in inventory that I didn't have to pay for, that they advertised to bring people to the store and they trained me so I could provide a living for my family. Do this instead of finding all the negatives at your job. Thank the people that help you. I would go around on the first of each month and thank the porters, and detailers, and fellow co-workers for their help the month before. If you treat the least of your co-workers as if they were the owners you will gain the respect of many.

Create a positive vocabulary with your customers. I will give you my top ten!

1) Excellent

2) Great

3) Super

4) Incredible

5) Done

6) Handled

7) I would be happy to

8) No problem

9) I understand

10) You don't have to ask me twice

Mirror your customer's body language and tone. If your customer speaks softly and slowly and you generally are loud and fast, you may want to mirror their tone and speech or you could freak them out. Body language is huge. After my first year in the business I stopped shaking hands in the greeting because I felt in some cases I was invading the buyer's space. Now if they immediately put out their hand I will shake it. But in a lot of cases you should be careful not to invade your customer's space and make them uncomfortable. I became a master at mirroring my client's body language and making them comfortable in the greeting. On occasion I would spend a ½ hour to an hour with a client and hadn't gotten their name; the reason was when I first got into selling I would shake their hand and introduce myself and they would give me their name, and inevitably by the time we got to my desk I already forgot their name. This was not because they were not important to me but because when I was meeting them, I was in fear. I had never met them, they had never met me, I wanted them to like me, I was afraid, and I'd forget their name. I started greeting customers by mirroring them and smiling, being friendly and making them comfortable.

Be prepared to overcome the "I'm just looking" response! You must be prepared to overcome objections even in the greeting. My personal favorite to this objection is to smile and say "Great, I have had 1000 customers and all of them started out just looking, are you looking for something bigger or smaller than your current vehicle?' This is super strong and generally breaks the ice; some people will smile or giggle but it almost always will draw a response. If you don't have a response for "just looking" get one, because you are losing sales every day- you give them a card and let them walk. Understand the buyer is there for a reason, most times to gain information, and his response is a defense mechanism to ward off unprofessional. This information I am sharing with you can be used on the sales floor, phone or internet. I am a firm believer that floor, phone or internet should be treated the same. Each scenario is different and obviously you can't mirror body language via the internet. However you can mirror language and tone. The same thing with the phone; you can mirror speech and tone. Don't think a customer can't see you smiling on the other end of the line. They can!

Be a Guru

Whether you are selling a product or service you must become an expert on that product or service. Because I sold cars, I will use it as my example. You must know every make and model, trim levels, packages, engines, Front wheel, all wheel, four wheel, rear wheel. Cloth or leather, moon roof, navigation, DVD. Wheel sizes, tire sizes, colors, safety features, suspensions. Exclusive features, fuel economy, transmission, warranty information, OnStar, Bluetooth, media, and every feature and benefit of every button on that car. You must train daily to stay up with technology as it is doubling every two years.

The worst thing that could happen is your customer knowing more about your product than you. You are the expert, so pride yourself on being an absolute expert on your product or service. Take advantage of as much training as possible. Buy the product yourself; this is a tremendous asset to use in your presentation. I own and use this product, Mr. Customer. What has more power than that?

You will also need to be aware of the competition for your product or service; it would be a great selling tool to know as much about your competition as you know about your product or service. The benefit of this information is to educate your customer as to why your product is superior to the competition.

Third party endorsements are extremely powerful to use in your presentation. Find out if your product or service has any awards or has been recognized by a third party like JD. Powers, Ward's Ten Best List, etc... Use this information in your delivery of information.

Find every exclusive feature your product offers and makes it unique versus its competitor and relay this information to the buyer. When demonstrating the feature make sure to give the customer the benefit. This is crucial to a great presentation. During my presentation of a car

I would mention that OnStar is an exclusive feature only offered by General Motors, and the benefit to you Mr. Customer is it gives you peace of mind before, during and after an accident god forbid that happens, but if it does there is someone on the line to assist you. Or if I were talking about remote start, although it is not an exclusive feature, I would always mention how it preconditions the car for your comfort, so if it is below 40 degrees and you use the remote start feature the car will automatically turn on your heated seats and set the temperature to 70 degrees. Notice the wording; always mention the feature and explain the benefit.

Objections

When I first started in the business I kept an objection notebook. I wrote down every objection that I heard from each customer. The funny thing that happened was that after a month I think I had written down every objection that I heard for the next 5 years. The objections started to repeat. I then developed overcoming objections for every objection that I heard and I tried to have five overcoming objections for each objection. When I figured this out my closing ratio increased exponentially. I would highly recommend you do the same. Each customer is different; for one customer you may only need two overcoming objections to get them to say yes, while others may take all five. Some you may use all five and still get a no, however at least you know you tried everything in your power to inspire them to say yes. "An objection is not a rejection; it is simply a request for more information." -Bo Bennett

Lastly, stay away from negative people. If you hang out with drug addicts the likelihood of you becoming a drug addict is very good, would you agree? So if I told you that you have a million dollar asset, would you protect it? If you hang around negative people the likelihood of you becoming negative is great. Start hanging with successful people and the more likely you will be successful. Surround yourself with like-minded people and observe what they do so you can imitate them. They won't mind. Imitation is the greatest form of flattery.

Hopefully you are enjoying this information because I feel like it is so rich and valuable. Most of the sales training on the market is done by professional sales trainers and there is nothing wrong with that, but I believe it is easy for someone not in the business to give you instruction on your business. But how much more pertinent is the information coming from someone who is currently using this material daily? This information I use daily and it works!

"Success is where preparation and opportunity meet." -Bobby Unser

Chapter 4

The Interview

"Knowledge is having the right answer. Intelligence is asking the right questions." -Unknown

In this chapter I will give you my keys to conducting a superior interview, and I promise some of the most compelling material yet to benefit you and your sales career.

The process where you gather information from your client starts with the interview. I recommend an interview be done in your seat, not on your feet. If you are in a retail environment, escort your customer to your desk. The term "follow me" works great because it puts you in control, or just walk to your desk; they will follow. I always have a pen and paper to write notes. Try not to be interrupted during this process as it makes your customer feel like they are not important. The customer you are with should always be your number one priority, always. Do not pick up the phone or greet another customer, don't get on your cell phone; it is disrespectful. Your job is to make your customer feel like they are the most important thing in your life right now.

The interview should not feel like an interrogation, it should feel like two neighbors talking in the front yard. I love using open ended questions that keep me in control of the conversation. If you can find out what inspires your customer you will be more likely to have them buy from you.

I used to believe building rapport was overrated, however after studying the definition of rapport I have changed my opinion. Rapport defined by the dictionary is," a close and harmonious relationship in which people understand each other's feelings or ideas and communicate well." Based on that definition there is nothing more important than building rapport. There is a difference between small talk and rapport building.

There are a few questions I like to start with that give me insight into my customers. One would be, tell me a little about your family? This is a great question to learn about your client and what inspires them. Once you ask the question, listen and take notes. Another question I like to ask, if it is a businessman or woman, is tell me how you got started in the business?

This type of questioning helps me build rapport by giving me the information on what is important to my buyer and how we may be alike.

I will generally follow up with a question like, what gets you out of bed in the morning. Or, what are you passionate about? These questions really get you the answers as to what inspires your client.

People are motivated by five needs: safety, variety, relationships, respect and purpose. Listening to the responses after these questions should give you insights as to what motivates your prospect. If I realize my customer's main need is safety and I was demonstrating a car, I would focus on safety features and warranty. If my customer's need was variety, maybe I would focus on the unique color and looks of the car. These principles can be used no matter what you are selling.

This information will be particularly important if you are in negotiations later and need leverage to convince them to buy from you. These questions are much different than, "What did you think of yesterday's football game?" This is the rapport I feel is overrated. Your customer is looking for information about your product and is far less likely to be amused by small talk about yesterday's football game, but most people will proudly tell you about their family or business, giving you insight into what is important to them.

People buy things for one reason: to solve a problem. Your job is to find what your customer's problem is so you can solve it. I was extremely successful selling customers when I found out about the last purchase of the product they were looking at. I wasn't even aware why. Then I figured it out; if you can find out what inspired your customer's last purchase of the product they are looking at you will have a much greater chance of selling them your product.

Questions are the keys to solving your customer's problem. So once I have gained personal information, and I find out how they bought the product previously, I focus on what they liked most about the product and what they did not like about the product. How many people will be using the product, how will the product be used?

Now if your customer has never used the product and you have shared all of the information about the product, I recommend you get to the why, what and how.

Why did you come in today and not last week or last month?

I'm curious, what made you decide on this particular product?

How is that important to you?

Why did you decide to meet with me?

What made you decide to do this now?

I was wondering, why would you make this kind of investment?

This is like Gold! I was working with a client on a $99,000 Cadillac Escalade ESV Platinum Edition, and he was trying to negotiate the price. I asked, "Why did you come in today?" He said, "You have the only ESV Platinum Edition in the color I am looking for." Then I asked, "Why now?" He said that he was getting ready to take a vacation with his family and he had been wanting to take the Escalade. I asked if he was paying cash or financing and to sign here and here. He never mentioned price again. We delivered the Escalade that day.

You were born with two ears and one mouth

The most important skill after asking great questions is to shut up and listen. I had to learn this. I am passionate and get excited for my customer. I would ask a great question and then think of my response and not really listen to my customer.

I lost many customers because I was not a good listener. You can become great at listening; ask your question and look your client in the eyes and genuinely listen to what he or she says. The reason most salespeople fail is they do not listen. If you get really good at asking the right questions and listening to what your client says, you will be really good at selling. Are you a good listener? Practice listening to others. How many times does your spouse or significant other say, are you even listening to me? How many times are they right? This skill will not only help you in sales but in your life!

We live in such a fast-paced society, in a 'me' world, where everyone is concerned about themselves. Listening is an underrated talent that brings extraordinary value not just for your customers, but your wife, kids, family and friends. Even people you just meet will be impressed with your ability to listen.

I was working with a Christian group recently selling a high end coaching program and when I called the prospect for our strategy session they were so grateful to have a live one on one with a real person, but even more excited to have someone truly listen to their story. With a very simple vision mapping question they would open up, telling me their life story in 30 to 45 minutes. This was extremely emotional and moving for me and them and I truly believe people are starving for someone to truly listen. Take this under-utilized tool and become great at it and you will change lives!

I hope you see the value in developing great questions for your product or service. Your questions will determine how successful you will be in sales. Don't interrogate. Make sure your customer feels important, and be genuine in helping others make the right decision. Stay in control by asking open ended questions. Find out what inspires your client. Listen, listen, and listen. Practice being a good listener. Take notes.

"Most people do not listen with the intent to understand; they listen with the intent to reply." -Stephen R. Covey

Chapter 5

The Power of Compromise

"No matter what the buyer says, states or demands, you should under no circumstances, ever disagree or make the buyer wrong or suggest their request is impossible." -Grant Cardone

In this chapter I will share with you the most powerful two and three words in the English language. I will also give the fundamental rule of selling and like the majority of what I am sharing with you in this book, not only does it apply to selling, but it applies to your success in life.

Always, always agree with the customer. This is the most neglected fundamental rule of selling. You can't be disagreeable and get agreement.

Try this with the next customer you greet—start an argument with them. Just see how much success you have selling them your product or service. Insult them, tell them they are stupid and they make no sense at all. Your probably saying that's crazy however whenever you get in disagreement with your customer that is what you are doing.

You should never expect someone to agree with you if you are disagreeing with them; it is virtually impossible. Look at your life, your friends, and your family members, the ones you are closest to; they are the ones you are in agreement with the most. If we like each other we have some type of agreement.

If you are trying to get agreement from a customer you must give agreement first. No matter how crazy or outlandish your customer is, just agree with them. This is different than the saying "the customer is always right". They are not always right. Right or wrong, though, don't fight the customer.

I can't tell you how many times I have been working with a client, and when we get to negotiations and share the figures they say I just want to wait. Early in my sales career as an amateur I did not know how to overcome that statement.

As a professional what I learned was to just agree. Waiting is a good idea, Mr. Customer. I did not push the customer away by disagreeing. Then I explain that waiting will not change that we are on the right product, that we can ensure programs, rebates and incentives today, that it is affordable, and by doing it today he can take advantage of the value the product brings immediately. Time is money wouldn't it be worth putting your focus on more important things that bring more value, rather than letting this linger? First I agreed, which gave me an opportunity to shift the customer's way of thinking.

In addition, very seldom does the deal ever get better! I have studied this, and in most cases the customer chases a payment. I recall a customer I had and he decided to wait. Three months went by and he came back. I finally said, "Look, I agreed with you last time you were in and I will stand by your decision today, but obviously you want to do this. You were here three months ago, and the only thing that happens when you wait is your trade goes down in price and the new car price goes up. Let's do this! Sign here and here." We signed him that day.

The thing I love most about the agreement principle is it not only works on customers, it works with friends and family. Some of my best results come from my kids. I used to argue with my kids about getting up and going to school. I started agreeing with them... "You know, when I was your age I used to hate waking up early and going to school too. Let's get up and get some breakfast, little man." The results of this principle are amazing. Try this in your life and I guarantee results.

Relax

I can remember in my first couple of years in sales one of the most terrifying statements was, "I just started looking and you are my first stop and I will be shopping you." My knees would start to shake, literally. "Wonderful I think that is a great idea, please just compare your experience here with what you get there. I promise if we can't come to an agreement on product and price I wouldn't expect you do business with me or us." When I learned this simple word track, it became flawless. A good portion of these customers never went anywhere else. They bought from me. Why? They left their guard down once I came into agreement and was able to speak their language.

People are looking for like-minded people. I was looking to have a cement driveway installed. I had three contractors give me estimates. The first contractor was a little unsure about if he could do what I wanted. The second contractor was like no problem, I can do exactly what you want and showed me how he could make it happen. The third contractor said what I wanted was not achievable. Although the second contractor was the most expensive, who do you think I ended up doing business with? Yes, contractor number two. Why? He was speaking my language! Even though he was $2000 dollars more, this driveway would be there for the next 30 years. I guarantee you, you can do the same thing. Get in agreement and speak their language; be a 'no problem' person.

Here is another example: a customer tells you they only have fifteen minutes. "Fifteen minutes is more than enough time!" Fifteen minutes turns into two hours and a delivery! Why does this work so well? Most sales consultants give them a card and see them on their way out. It is so different from how most other unprofessional sales consultants handle time limitations. Your customer is surprised and realizes you're a professional.

Nothing will build confidence with your customer more than your ability to agree. Your ability to agree is more critical than all other rules of selling, including your ability to close. If you disagree with your customer you may never get to the close

The Two and Three Most Powerful Words in the English Language

Do you want to learn how to stop an argument between you and someone else? Just say these two words. I Agree. It doesn't take two people to agree, just one. Who can argue with that? If you just say I Agree, argument over. If you want to continue an argument with someone, just tell them they're wrong.

Imagine you are in an argument with your spouse or girlfriend; there is no easier way to end the argument than by using these three words. You are right. A customer that is upset with you: "You are right, Mr. Customer. I agree with you. What can I do to make this better?" But if you tell him he is wrong you will be adding fuel to the fire.

A customer tells you, "It's too much money." "You're right, it is a lot of money. Everyone that has bought this product has said it's a lot of money, which is why you should get it today so you can get a return on your investment right away."

Agreement is the best way to getting your own way! Practice using these simple words not only in sales, but in your personal life, and watch the amazing results.

"If two or three agree on a common purpose, nothing is impossible." - Jim Rohn

Chapter Six

The Value Proposition

"Price is what you pay. Value is what you get." Warren Buffet

What is your opinion on money? Do you believe you have to work hard for money? Do you have difficulty parting with your money? In this Chapter I will breakdown the money myth. This is a very important part to every sale as people are very funny when it comes to money. Your buyer can act weird, make excuses, stall or even exaggerate the truth when it comes to parting with their money. A professional sales consultant knows how to handle stalls and objections and still stay focused on the deal; they know how to persevere and not use pressure with the customer.

If you have issues parting with your money, you will have a hard time getting others to part with their money. Money is more a mental issue than anything else. If you grew up in a household like mine where it was said that, "you must work hard for your money", your mental programming will make it so you believe making money takes a lot of hard work. You must change that programming. There is no shortage of money, however there is a shortage of salespeople who know how to earn it. The less possessive you are with money, the more money you will see. The more you give and realize money is to be used, not possessed, the more money you will receive. Your buyer will tell you they "can't afford it!" Absolutely they can; that is why we have financial institutions.

Second Money

When I was corporate training for the auto group I worked for I put a tremendous amount of effort into training consultants on the fact that second money is easier than first money. Sales consultants are so insecure about introducing additional products after they get their customers to say yes. They don't want to jeopardize the deal. But in fact, the second money is easier than the first money because it reaffirms their decision to buy.

I came across this fact when I was selling a truck. I worked several hours with a customer on making a decision on a truck in which he tried to pinch every penny out of the deal. I turned my computer screen to him and while I was copying his information I offered him to look at the available accessories for his truck. To my surprise he bought an additional several thousand dollars in accessories. I then presented him a warranty and tire protection. He bought everything I presented.

This made me think of my own buying habits. When I go to buy a suit, I generally don't just buy the suit but also a tie and maybe cufflinks, and sometimes socks and shoes. Once I figured out this phenomenon I became one of the highest grossing back end sales consultants for the rest of my career. In some cases I would make more money off of the back end products than I would the sale of the car or truck. People love to showboat; people want more, not less. Second money is for the professional who wants to take his game to the next level. Remember, the second purchase reaffirms the first purchase.

This is an incredibly powerful technique that I found works best when you get the initial yes; just ask your customer about additional items and watch as the floodgates open to your aftermarket ability to sell.

The Money Myth

The most common misconception in sales is that if you have a less expensive price that you would sell more of your product or service. This is absolutely untrue. The greatest example I can give to you comes from one of my mentors, Grant Cardone, who had scheduled a sales seminar in Detroit, Michigan. A sales representative for Grant had mentioned to him that he felt that if he lowered the price of admission for the seminar that he could sell more prospects on the seminar. Detroit had always been one of the most-attended seminar markets.

As much as Grant disagreed with the sales representative he agreed to lower the price, however, he would not allow the sales representative to do a full presentation as they were offering the seminar at 1/10 the normal cost.

This seminar had the lowest participation of any seminar that Mr. Cardone had ever done in twenty years. It did not even cover the cost of his airfare and sales commissions didn't cover the cost of mailers. When Grant asked the audience why they thought so few people came, they said that they didn't think he would actually be there but that it would be a video feed. If the price is too inexpensive, people will not see value in the product.

After this experiment he doubled his price and attendance at future seminars increased 100%.

Price is only an issue if you haven't built enough value. If you have built enough value, price will never be the issue. I have studied this extensively and will honestly tell you if price is the objection it is mostly a stall or a complaint, not a valid objection if you have built value. How do you know if you have built enough value? You must go back to the interview and if done properly, you have the information to solve the problem for your customer. And if price is a valid objection then you have not built enough value in your product or service so that your customer is willing to part with their money. Your customer is not confident enough or does not love your product enough to solve their problem. I continually think back to the boss I had early in my career who told me that you are on the wrong car, it's too much car. I was new to the business but one thing I knew early on is a customer will not buy something they do not love! It is virtually impossible to sell someone something if they are not head over heels about your product or service.

I developed a great question for when I got back from a test drives with a customer and the question is, "On a scale of 1 to 10, where do you find yourself on these cars?" I try always to give more than one option for test drives. I will tell you I have never sold someone who was an 8 or less, why? If a customer is an 8 or above you may sway them on different thing: rate, payment or terms. I have never had a price objection if my customer gave me a ten. Does that make sense? You could use this same questioning no matter what product or service you offer.

I have found in most cases that if a customer who can afford to buy my product or service is objecting to money, the customer is not afraid of the money, they are afraid of making a decision, the wrong decision. You must be able to put to rest what your customer's unspoken objection really is, like, is it the right product? Are the terms agreeable? Is there a better product available? Are you the right salesperson and will your company provide the right service? Have you provided the customer with all of the necessary information to make an educated decision? Should I lease or buy? Would I be better served paying cash or financing? Am I making the right decision?

When you have answered all of the above questions I can assure you price will not be an issue! The extent to which you understand and believe this truth will perfectly determine your success in overcoming price as an objection. Truly, it is almost never price.

It Is Never the Customers Fault, It's ALWAYS Your Fault

The more you can come to grips with this fact, the better off you will be. I developed a saying for when a customer said, "I'm sorry." "Mr. Customer, no apology necessary as it is not your fault you're not buying, but mine!"

Never, ever, ever is it the customer. There are times when I am with the buyer and price is the objection where I will close the door to my office and say, "I must not have done a good enough job with demonstration, presentation and explanation of features and benefits because I know if I had done so price would not be the objection. I realize that I am always the one who stops the sale, not the customer."

Everyone has had a loved one who has passed away and there is no doubt in my mind you have said or heard this statement: "I would give up everything or anything if I could have saved them." If they could have bought a cure, there is no uncertainty in my mind that no amount of money would have been unreasonable and they would have found a way to get the money. If the love is great enough and the cure is bold enough, money would not be the issue. When you realize that it is love, not money, your results will be your reward.

I have literally had hundreds of my customers thank me for staying in the deal, not giving up, and for giving them the necessary push to buy my product. The level of confidence you can exude in your product or service that convinces your customer it is the right thing to do will determine your level of success.

Give Options

One of my greatest assets in overcoming objections is to not have any. I believe that giving options is the undisputed way to eliminate objections. When you give a client options they find what they love. 86% of customers buy something other than what they came in for. Why not give them options to find what they love? I recommend you do this for product, finance and aftermarket products as well. Finance departments have done a great job with this by creating a menu for aftermarket products, realizing a customer is more likely to buy something when given more than one option.

I was working with a customer for a few hours one night and I was in my first year or so. We did not come to an agreement on a car. He left and on my drive home I thought I should have offered him a used car! It was too late in the evening to call that night so I called him first thing in the morning, and he had bought a used car from one of my competitors. This was a great learning lesson for me, and I vowed always to give options so this would never happen again. I will tell you as a professional in sales there is nothing worse than not exhausting all of your options, only to have someone steal your commission because you missed this vital selling point.

I also discovered another critical piece of information in giving your buyer options.

When in negotiations, a customer has a price objection to your product. Your instinct will have you move down in product as your customer's objection is money, so your first inclination would be to model down to get a less expensive price. I can unequivocally tell you that is incorrect. I have learned that the customer's objection of money was due to the fact that there was not enough value in the product; most of my success has come with moving up in product. The customer will pay more if you build enough value. If I am working with a customer on a cloth interior with the bare minimum equipment and the objection is price, I would move to a leather model with a sunroof. I would also model down if available or show a used car as well. In a great majority of examples like this the customer will bump themselves up, not down.

Remember, if they love the product money will not be an issue; they will find a way to get the money.

Success. If it is going to Be, It is Up To Me!

I wanted to develop an easy to read book with five game changing strategies that you could implement immediately to change your career, but more importantly, change your life. I believe that each strategy I have shared in this book can be used to increase your sales. I also believe you can use these powerful techniques to change your life, create freedom financially and also produce freedom to do the things you want and love. I enjoy watching my kids play sports and I want to be able to go to every event that I can because one day they will be grown and gone, and so will be the time I had to enjoy them while they are young. I believe many of you reading this book would love to have the freedom to do the same thing. People have learned to settle; they had a dream and life beat the dream out of them.

I want you to rekindle the dream you had when you were young.

Ask a bunch of ten year olds what their dream is and every one of them has an answer. Ask a bunch of thirty year olds what their dream is, and how many of them can even answer the question? I truly believe it is never too late to get your passion back.

There is a talent you are born with that makes you different than everyone else; it is yours, it was made for you. Our job and duty is to either live with it or die with it. When you figure out what it is, you will not sleep to dream it, but wake to live it. You do not have to go through a major life crisis to start living your dream today. The cemetery is a graveyard for ideas and dreams that never came to fruition; don't let yours be one of them.

"I've learned people will forget what you said, people will forget what you did, but people will never forget the way you made them feel." - Maya Angelou

"If you want something bad enough to go out and fight for it,

To work day and night for it, to give up your time, your peace and sleep for it...

If all that you dream and scheme is about, and life seems useless without it... if you

Gladly sweat for it and fret for it and plan for it and lose all your terror of the opposition for it...

If you simply go after that thing that you want with all your capacity, strength and sagacity, faith

Hope and confidence and stern pertinacity... if neither poverty, famine, nor gout, sickness nor

Pain, of body and brain, can keep you away from the thing that you want... if dogged and grim

You beseech and best it, with the help of God, YOU WILL GET IT!"

"Things as They Are" -Berton Braley

I wanted to end my book with the most inspirational quote I have ever read. I had never heard this quote until after suffering my heart attack and it inspired me to find my true passion and purpose in life, and hopefully my book will do the same for you. Look for my series of inspirational books and my Udemy course coming soon.

"In order to get something you never had you must do what you have never done!" Thomas Jefferson

About The Author

Bill Feudale is a professional Sales Consultant, Life and Business Coach. Bill has a degree in Business Management and Marketing. He has been a successful entrepreneur—owning a successful Automotive Retail Business that led him in a career in the Automotive Sales Industry. Bill worked his way up from a detailer to General Sales Manager for an automotive group he worked for in Michigan. Bill has spent 12 years in retail sales were he was recognized by General Motors as Top Performer in Outstanding Product knowledge and Customer Service. He has also been a three time People Choice Award winner for the Milford Times Salesperson of the Year. Bill has also been a corporate trainer, Sales Manager and General Sales Manager. Bill is the ultimate survival story often comparing his life to the movie Eight Mile before Eight Mile and he did not know how to sing. Bill enjoys coaching youth sports and is on the finance committee at his church. Bill is the father of three wonderful children. He is a Christian a coach and a leader. After suffering a heart attack in August of 2014 he has been dedicated to his passion in life. His purpose is to help others achieve their dream life without having to go through a life crisis to get there.

Contacts

Bill Feudale email – bill@beawinnerinlife.com

Website: www.beawinnerinlife.com

Youtube: www.youtube.com/channel/UCcBBgZ6y56gojlN1BkbXZ1w

LinkedIn.com: www.LinkedIn.com/billfeudale

Facebook: https://www.facebook.com/beawinnerinlife

www.ingramcontent.com/pod-product-compliance
Lightning Source LLC
Chambersburg PA
CBHW070939180526
45168CB00003B/1108